Words: A Journey

Ignatius Maximus John and Grace Lalrinpari Hauzel

Published by Gumby Publishers, 2023.

Published by Gumby Publishers,
36 Saint John's Place
Freeport 11520-4618
New York, USA

Airhub 1425, UBX 6 Poyle Trading Estate,
Colndale Road, Colnbrook
Slough SL30AA
Berkshire, United Kingdom

Table of Contents

Mellifluous 1

Apricity 2

Rakuyou 4

Retrouvailles...6

Hitoritabi..8

Luftmensch 10

Raconteur 12

Sirimiri 13

Rimjhim.. 15

Petrichor 16

Morii 18

Fernweh.. 20

Resfeber.. 22

Nefelibata 24

Smultronställe.. 26

Dustsceawung.. 28

Nakakapagpabagabag.. 30

Brontide 32

Aesthete 33

Sophrosyne 35

Elysian 36

Mångata 38

Koi No Yokan 39

Abditory 41

Flawsome 42

Datsuzoku... 44

Vacilando 45

Komorebi.. 47

Metanoia... 48

Peregrinate 50

Perambulate 52

Peripatetic 54
Shinrin-yoku 55
Shinrabansho 56
Gadabout 57
Hiraeth 58
Toska 59
Dépaysement 60
Dès Vu 61
Cynefin 62
Safarnama 63
Saudade 64
Yūgen 65
Wabi-Sabi 66
Ukiyo 67
Ikigai 68
Apprivoise 69
Còsagach 70
Ataraxia 71
Absquatulate 73

Grace Lalrinpari Hauzel is an enthusiastic budding writer who has been writing short stories and poetries since she was 6 years old. She manifested her views on life, emphasizing the enigmatic and arduous journey which are often thought provoking. Grace writes about nature, human emotions and divine love, using human love as an allegory. Grace is notorious for being a sleepyhead, most importantly a blithesome person. Her literary skills have gained recognition and have been awarded various awards.

Ignatius Maximus John is a poet who has been writing for decades. His poems are filled with deep emotion and personal experiences that make his work relatable to many people. He writes about love, heartbreak, and the everyday struggles of life. He often writes about his love for the beauty in nature, which makes his work a beautiful read. He has been published in many magazines and journals, and has won many awards for his work.

# About The Book

Words: A Journey is a poetry book by Ignatius Maximus John and Grace Lalrinpari Hauzel. The book is a collection of poems that explore the power of words to express emotions, to connect with others, and to make sense of the world.

The poems in Words: A Journey are written from a variety of perspectives, and they cover a wide range of topics. The poems are both lyrical and thought-provoking, and they offer a unique perspective on the power of words.

Words: A Journey is a beautiful and thought-provoking collection of poems. It is a book that will stay with you long after you have finished reading it.

Preface

Yes, life is a journey filled with different emotions and experiences. We experience joy, sadness, anger, fear, love, and many other emotions throughout our lives. We also have a variety of experiences, both good and bad. These experiences shape us into the people we are.

The journey of life is not always easy. There will be times when we experience challenges and setbacks. But there will also be times when we experience joy and fulfillment. It is important to remember that the journey of life is not about avoiding challenges or pain. It is about learning and growing from our experiences, both good and bad.

The journey of life is also about making choices. We have the choice to focus on the negative aspects of our lives, or we can choose to focus on the positive. We have the choice to be grateful for what we have, or we can choose to be envious of what others have. The choices we make will determine the quality of our journey.

We believe that the journey of life is a gift. It is an opportunity to learn and grow, to experience joy and sorrow, to make a difference in the world. We are grateful for the journey of life, and we're excited to see what the future holds.

Ignatius Maximus John & Grace Lalrinpari Hauzel

Mellifluous

In realms where words dance and dreams take flight,
A symphony in syllables, a stroke of light,
There lies a tapestry of sounds untamed,
A melodic rhythm, mellifluous and untamed.
Mellifluous, whispers on the wind, so sweet,
A soothing balm for hearts that must retreat,
Through dulcet tones, melodies cascade,
A river of harmony, a serenade.
Like honeyed nectar dripping from a flower,
Mellifluous tones possess a gentle power,
They sway our spirits with celestial grace,
And weave a spell, embracing every space.
The lark's lament, a melancholic plea,
Or laughter's trill, pure joy set free,
Each note a brush painting life's grand design,
Mellifluous, the language of divine.
Through mortal lips or nature's vibrant throng,
Mellifluous whispers linger, sweet and strong,
They stir emotions deep within our core,
And in their embrace, we yearn for more.
So let us pause, and with attentive ear,
Imbibe the symphony that speaks so clear,
For in mellifluous whispers, we shall find,
A symphony that stirs both heart and mind.

Apricity

In the bleakness of winter's cold embrace,
Where melancholy deeds are interlaced,
There shines a word, a notion to hold dear,
A gentle warmth through the frost to endear.
Apricity, like whispers on the frosty air,
A tender kiss of sunlight, so rare,
Painting golden hues upon frozen earth,
A respite from winter's icy mirth.
In this grace, souls find solace and ease,
As nature's touch fills barren hearts with peace.
Apricity, the glowing ember of hope,
A balm for weary souls forced to cope.
It speaks of woven memories in the snow,
Of whispered secrets that only treescapes know,
Its essence like a dance of winter's bride,
A gentle nudge, a sigh we cannot hide.
For in this fragile warmth, a fire awakes,
Stories unfold in each sunlit snowflake,
Transporting minds to dreams of summer's bliss,
Where apricity lives, in eternal kiss.
Ode to apricity, let your essence persist,
In the hearts of those who have yearned and missed,
Your touch, a reminder of life's tender grace,
A promise that darkness will soon embrace.
So let us revel in the warmth you bring,
And let our souls be touched by your sweet sting,
Apricity, an eternal melody,

A gift to cherish for all eternity.

Rakuyou

In the land of blossoms, where the whispers of time reside,
Lies Rakuyou, a realm where nature and beauty coincide.
Autumn paints its strokes of fiery gold, fierce and bold,
A tapestry woven by seasons, captivating stories untold.
As the sun adorns the horizon with its warm embrace,
Leaves dance upon the breeze, in a gentle, graceful chase.
Rustling melodies fill the air, a symphony with no end,
Nature's harmonious cadence, a song the heart can comprehend.
Oh, Rakuyou, your essence bewitches and beguiles,
Transcending mortal bounds with your enchanting smiles.
The mountains rise, guardians of tales, standing tall,
Echoing the whispers of legends, captivating one and all.
Through tranquil gardens, strolling under the pale moon's glow,
Lost souls find solace, seeking solace in your ebb and flow.
Meditating by serene lakes, reflecting dreams in its ripples,
One's spirit wanders freely, embracing life's sacred principles.
In the tranquil stillness, where time becomes a fleeting guest,
The soul finds respite, finding solace from the unrest.
Rakuyou, I stand in awe, for you hold a magic profound,
A sanctuary for weary hearts, where true serenity is found.
In every falling leaf, a story unfurls, a moment to share,
Speaking of impermanence, reminding us to cherish and care.
Ah, Rakuyou, your beauty ignites a flame within our souls,
A beacon of hope, guiding us towards serenity's gentle folds.
So let us wander these ancient paths, and with reverence bow,
Rakuyou, your allure forever ingrained in our hearts, we vow.
For in your embrace, we find solace, we find release,

And through the seasons of life, our spirits find eternal peace.

Retrouvailles

In the twilight's gentle hue,
As dusk blankets the world anew,
A whispered longing softly stirs,
As Retrouvailles leaves hearts astir.
In realms where time's hands intertwine,
Where destinies align, divine,
Two souls diverged, each on their way,
Destined to meet again, someday.
Lost amidst life's winding maze,
They seek solace in distant days,
Memories woven, fragile thread,
Leading them to where past meets ahead.
Retrouvailles, the fateful reunion,
A balm for hearts plagued with confusion,
Through life's ebbs and flows they find,
Their souls forever intertwined.
Eyes lock, a flicker ignited,
Echoes of laughter once delighted,
A touch familiar, resonant as the sea,
A whispered promise, forever set free.
In this sacred moment, time stands still,
The universe conspires, an artist's skill,
Their hearts entwined, harmonious so,
A symphony of love, a melodic glow.
Retrouvailles, a dance of souls aflame,
Rekindling love that has no name,
A testament to fate's gentle hand,

Two hearts eternally bound in love's command.
So let the stars bear witness, above,
To this wondrous gift, a miracle of love,
As Retrouvailles gifts lovers might,
An eternal bond, forever alight.

Hitoritabi

In vast lands of solitude, where shadows roam,
A solitary soul takes a path unknown.
Hitoritabi, the journey of one's embrace,
A tale of self-discovery, a sacred space.
Through veils of uncertainty, she treads alone,
Seeking solace in the whispers of the unknown.
Each step, a waltz with uncertainty's embrace,
Hitoritabi, a dance of grace and endless chase.
The world is her canvas, her footprints, a song,
Leaving traces of dreams as she journeys along.
Her heart, a compass, guiding her day and night,
Hitoritabi, a tapestry woven from moonlight.
In nights hushed by stars, she gazes at the skies,
Visions of fleeting beauty reflected in her eyes.
A tapestry of emotions, woven deep within,
Hitoritabi, a symphony of the soul's longing.
In the depths of silence, her spirit finds its voice,
Echoing through the valleys, inviting a timeless choice.
With every passing moment, she unravels the unknown,
Hitoritabi, a journey where her spirit has grown.
A melody of solitude guides her weary feet,
Where echoes of existence and purpose meet.
Hitoritabi, a pilgrimage of self-rebirth,
The poet's greatest muse, the Universe's dearth.
So let her wander, let her dance upon life's stage,
As her heart composes melodies that resonate.
Hitoritabi, a poem etched in the sands of time,

A quest for truth, a poetic rhythm so sublime.

Luftmensch

In the realm where dreams take flight,
Where reality blends with whimsical might,
Exists a being of ethereal essence,
A wanderer without a physical presence.
Behold! The Luftmensch, a soul adrift,
Lost in a world they struggle to lift,
Tangled in wisps of poetic thought,
With journeys in words, their solace sought.
Through the corridors of a boundless mind,
They wander untethered, seeking to find,
The beauty hidden amidst the mundane,
Weaving tales of wonder, poetry's domain.
Their spirit dances in the realm of air,
Suspended in time, without a care,
Unburdened by the weight of earthly things,
The Luftmensch soars on enchanted wings.
They breathe in syllables, exhale verse,
A humble vessel for the universe,
Conjuring imagery, painting skies anew,
Immersed in the magic that words imbue.
With pens as compasses, they navigate,
Crafting verses, their essence innate,
Conveying sentiments, both fierce and mild,
Elevating dreams, leaving hearts beguiled.
But within this whimsy, an ache lies hidden,
For the Luftmensch yearns to be unfettered,
To taste the world they paint with words,

To journey beyond their pen's confines, unheard.
So, let us honor the Luftmensch's plight,
For in their imaginings, truths ignite,
They remind us, with their ethereal art,
Of the endless potential within our own heart.

Raconteur

In the realm of tales and tales untold,
Lies a figure with stories to behold.
A weaver of words, a master of art,
The raconteur, possessing a captivating heart.
With a voice that dances upon the air,
They capture our minds, taking us elsewhere.
Through whispers and gestures, a grand display,
They ensnare our thoughts, leading us astray.
Their words, like jewels, glisten and gleam,
Bringing dreams and memories into our realm.
They paint scenes of love and of despair,
And lift us to heights beyond compare.
In ancient taverns, their tales take flight,
Guiding us through the depths of the night.
From laughter to tears, their stories sway,
Allowing us to ponder, to reflect, and to play.
But it's not just words that they impart,
For the raconteur speaks straight to the heart.
With every syllable, they touch our souls,
Leaving behind footprints, like enchanted scrolls.
So, let us cherish the raconteur's gift,
For in their stories, our spirits uplift.
They bridge the gaps, connect us all,
And through their art, humanity stands tall.

Sirimiri

In the whispers of a tender rain,
A subtle dance upon the windowpane,
Sirimiri gracefully descends,
Caressing the Earth, where it mends.
A gentle mist, a silent hush,
Bathed in drops, like a morning blush,
Sirimiri weaves a tapestry rare,
Stirring emotions, light as air.
Each tiny droplet, a liquid pearl,
Unveiling secrets in this watery swirl,
A symphony of soft, melodic notes,
Where nature's poetry gently floats.
The raindrops kiss the thirsty ground,
Reviving life, in a delicate sound,
Nourishing roots, awakening dreams,
Sirimiri falls, weaving mystical streams.
Embracing tender petals with care,
Washing away worries, burdens to bear,
In this ethereal shower, hearts find relief,
As nature's tears bring solace, brief.
Sirimiri whispers tales untold,
A gentle hymn, both soft and bold,
With each raindrop, a story unfurled,
A symphony played in this watery world.
Let the murmur of Sirimiri enchant,
An invitation to pause, to take a chance,
To dance with nature, bathe in its grace,

And find solace in this rain-kissed embrace.

Rimjhim

In the realm of rains, where dreams descend,
There dances a melody, sweet and soft, my friend.
It whispers on rooftops and drips from the sky,
Rimjhim, the divine symphony, oh how it can make you sigh.
Its gentle patter, like a lover's gentle touch,
Caresses the earth, as it yearns for such.
With every drop, a rhythm forms,
An enchanting serenade, in nature's arms.
Rimjhim, the dancer, swirling with grace,
Creating a tapestry, where emotions interlace.
In each raindrop, a tale unfolds,
Of lovers separated, and desires untold.
The symphony swells, as thunder finds its voice,
Echoing through the heavens, it chooses to rejoice.
Rimjhim, the orchestrator, conducts the song of the skies,
Melting hearts, with its tender lullabies.
And as the rain subsides, it leaves behind,
A world bathed, in stories undefined.
Rimjhim, the poet, with its touch divine,
Leaves us yearning for more, lost in its rhyme.
So, let us embrace this gift from above,
Let Rimjhim serenade our souls, with love.
For in its presence, we find solace and release,
In the poetry of raindrops, our hearts find peace.

Petrichor

In the midst of a desolate drought,
When arid whispers dance around,
Petrichor emerges, breaking the spell,
A symphony of earth's salvation, profound.
Gently, raindrops kiss the parched ground,
Unveiling the ancient elixir, untamed,
With each drop's descent, a sigh resounds,
A melody of petrichor, passion unchained.
From the soil's embrace, a fragrance awakes,
Aromas mingling, nature's sweet embrace,
Anointment of life, a union of earth and sky,
Petrichor's enchantment, a gift of grace.
Invisible tendrils caress the senses,
Memories awaken, from depths unseen,
Childhood dreams and distant landscapes,
Petrichor's essence, a portal between.
Released in rhythm, petrichor paints,
A tapestry of emotions, raw and profound,
Whispering tales of eternal change,
Stories of life, lost and found.
In petrichor's sweet embrace, we find,
Renewal in the early morning rain,
As nature weeps its tender tears,
Reviving spirits, healing pain.
Oh, petrichor, faithful friend,
Your perfume a balm for weary hearts,
In your embrace, we find solace,

In your whispers, new life starts.

Morii

In the darkest depths of night, Morii does abide,
A spirit ancient, yet ever so alive.
With ethereal grace, she weaves her lustrous thread,
Unraveling our fears, as dreams take their stead.
Her touch, like whispers upon our weary souls,
Awakening dormant desires, making them whole.
She paints the sky in hues of soft moonlight,
Infusing hope in our hearts, in the dead of night.
Morii, the harbinger of dreams that mend,
Unfolding realms of magic, without end.
In her cocoon of shadows, she gently weaves,
A tapestry of solace, where the heart finds ease.
Through the veil of slumber, she takes our hand,
Guiding us to lands where dreams expand.
We dance with stars, every worry fades away,
Lost in the vast embrace of a celestial ballet.
She captures fleeting moments, in timeless art,
Creating landscapes where love will never depart.
Her spectral brushstrokes paint the world aglow,
An enchanting symphony that only she can bestow.
But beware, oh mortal, when Morii does appear,
For dreams can lure, and reality ensnares.
Yet in her delicate touch, a secret lies,
That dreams, if cherished, can make hearts arise.
So heed her whispers in the hush of the night,
Embrace her gift, let dreams take flight.
For in Morii's realm, where hopes do reside,

She breathes life into souls, and forever abides.

Fernweh

In the heart's quiet chambers, a whisper lingers,
A yearning that ignites the soul's gentle fires;
It beckons with a cosmic pull, strong and true,
A longing for the foreign, for adventures anew.
Fernweh, they call it, a wistful melody,
That resonates deep within, a wild symphony;
It seeks unknown horizons, uncharted lands,
It yearns for distant shores and shifting sands.
In dreams, we traverse across distant skies,
Leaving footprints on mountains that pierce the clouds;
We wander through alleys with secrets untold,
In search of stories yet to unfold.
Through the untamed wilderness we roam,
By rivers that sing ancient tales of their own;
Guided by stars, we embrace the unknown,
With each step, we find a piece of our own.
Fernweh, a love affair with the unseen,
With cultures, languages, and visions yet unclean;
It pulls at the core, urges us to explore,
To absorb the essence of worlds we adore.
With hunger in our hearts, we journey far and wide,
Unweaving boundaries, embracing life's stride;
Fernweh, a compass to navigate our dreams,
Where wanderlust and destiny perfectly scheme.
So let us seize the moments, cradle the fleeting,
For in the pursuit of Fernweh, we find meaning;
A call to wander beyond borders' confine,

To discover ourselves in places divine.
As the wind whispers tales of distant shores,
We answer Fernweh's call, as our spirits soar;
In the poetry of travel, we etch our legacy,
Embracing Fernweh's magic, forever free.

Resfeber

In the depths of a restless heart, it stirs,
A whispering call that cannot be ignored,
Resfeber, the wild spirit of wanderlust,
Ignites the flame, longing to explore.
Through the weary bones and tired eyes,
Resfeber dances, a vibrant surge,
A symphony of longing, an untamed cry,
Beckoning the weary soul to emerge.
Like rivers that flow from distant lands,
Resfeber courses through the traveler's veins,
Tugging at the core, like shifting sands,
Compelling the feet, where adventure reigns.
It whispers tales of distant shores,
Of mountain peaks that defy the sky,
Of ancient cultures and untrodden floors,
Of horizons where dreams dare to fly.
Every heartbeat echoes the resounding drum,
As Resfeber paints visions both vast and grand,
Unveiling treasures yet to be undone,
In realms unknown, untouched by human hand.
Beneath the moonlit skies, it sets ablaze,
Flames of curiosity, burning bright,
Fueling the yearning in untamed ways,
For journeys that transcend both space and time.
Resfeber, oh sweet and restless spark,
Ignite our souls, unbind these worldly chains,
Lead us to depths unknown, through light and dark,

As we surrender to your wild refrains.
Let our spirits soar through uncharted skies,
Casting aside fears that would hold us tight,
For in Resfeber's embrace, we realize,
The world is but a canvas, ours to ignite.

Nefelibata

In realms where dreams take flight, behold Nefelibata,
A soul untethered, dancing with the clouds,
With nimble steps, she weaves a tapestry of wonder,
A poet's muse, enchanting, never subdued.
Her spirit, free as the wind, wandering afar,
Through realms unseen, where imagination thrives,
She dwells amidst the whispers of celestial beings,
A silent symphony, where dreams come alive.
Nefelibata, a wanderer of worlds untold,
With every footstep, she paints stars anew,
Her heart a kaleidoscope of vivid hues,
And in her eyes, the secrets of the universe unfold.
She strays through fields of blossoms and wild meadows,
A pilgrim of the infinite, her mind takes flight,
Feathers of inspiration gracefully adorn her soul,
As she tethered to nothing, lives in endless delight.
Her path, a labyrinth of constellations unknown,
She navigates the depths of ethereal glow,
Scribing ballads of love, loss, and longing,
In verses pure, like streams that gracefully flow.
Nefelibata, an emissary of ethereal realms,
Her verses carry echoes of forgotten tales,
Through her words, emotions bloom like flowers in spring,
And sorrow dissipates, as hope eternally prevails.
Breathe in her poems, dear reader, and be transported,
To transcendent realms where dreams find their way,
For Nefelibata, the poetess of boundless horizons,

Invites us all to embrace the magic of today.

Smultronställe

In the hidden depths of memories untold,
Lies a sacred place, an enchanting folklore,
Where time stands still, and worries unfold,
Oh, Smultronställe, the heart's evermore.
Amongst the whispers of silence that carry,
Here nature's symphony, a gentle embrace,
Where the soul finds solace, moments merry,
In this haven of dreams, a tranquil space.
Sunlit meadows paint the canvas divine,
Vibrant wildflowers dance in rhythmic sway,
Their fragrance a lullaby, a sweet serpentine,
Echoing stories of love and dreams' ballet.
With every step, on paths of ancient lore,
I lose myself in this paradise's maze,
The stillness within, and wonders galore,
As heartfelt whispers guide my wandering ways.
The soft kiss of the breeze caresses my cheek,
As the sun rainbows through the forest's veil,
I reach out to touch the dreams I seek,
In this Smultronställe, where spirits prevail.
In fields of dew-kissed strawberries, we unite,
A taste of heaven on a crimson delight,
A stolen moment, tender and infinite,
A sweet symphony, singing love's rhapsody, right.
Oh, Smultronställe, you hold secrets untold,
A sanctuary where hearts find respite,
A refuge for wanderers, both young and old,

Where dreams flourish, and souls reunite.

Dustsceawung

In the realm of dusty dreams and hidden tales,
Where shadows dance and whispers prevail,
There lies a state of mind, a timeless sting,
A melancholy called Dustsceawung.
Is it a tremor of sorrow or subtle despair?
This spectral waltz with secrets laid bare,
A yearning for what has long since passed,
Now scattered like ashes, memories amassed.
In the breath of ages, forgotten and worn,
Aching souls whisper, their hearts forlorn,
They speak of aching beauty, elusive and fleeting,
Of dreams unfulfilled, hopes slowly retreating.
Through the tendrils of time, they softly cry,
Seeking solace, wondering why,
The dust of dreams clings to their souls,
In shadows cast, where solemnity unfolds.
Yet amidst this haze, a glimmering light,
A kindling spark, piercing the night,
For Dustsceawung bears both gentle pain,
And the seeds of resilience, hope to sustain.
In this poetic dance, hearts will renew,
The particles of life, retouched, imbued,
For in Dustsceawung, there lies a chance,
To rise from the ashes, to embrace the dance.
So let these verses caress your heart,
Awakening emotions, each line a dart,
And may you find solace, dear reader, dear friend,

In the bittersweet symphony of Dustsceawung's blend.

Nakakapagpabagabag

In the depth of the ethereal night,
Where shadows dance and thoughts take flight,
There lies a word that lingers still,
Nakakapagpabagabag, it does instill.
It whispers sweetly, a subtle tease,
Unleashing demons, disturbing peace,
It wraps around the heart so tight,
A restless turmoil, an endless fight.
Nakakapagpabagabag, what does it mean?
A trembling soul, a shattered dream,
It speaks of restlessness, anxiety's embrace,
A haunting presence, obscuring grace.
In the silent echoes of a troubled mind,
Nakakapagpabagabag, we often find,
A chaotic dance of worry and fear,
A storm within, shedding countless tears.
Yet amidst the terrors that this word can bring,
Hope and resilience forever sing,
For the human spirit, unwavering and strong,
Can face these trials, and rise beyond.
So embrace the unease, let it ignite,
A flame within, burning ever bright,
For Nakakapagpabagabag may try to ensnare,
But we shall find strength, and breathe in air.
In the face of uncertainty, we shall live,
Every ounce of our being, we shall give,
And through the darkest nights, we'll find a way,

To conquer Nakakapagpabagabag and seize the day.

Brontide

In the realm where thunder's mighty roar resides,
A symphony of clouds swirls and collides,
Brontide, the essence of Nature's grand refrain,
A conductor's baton, orchestrating without strain.
Oh, Brontide, your echoes fill the boundless sky,
A celestial drumscape, where galaxies lie,
With each resounding boom, hearts start to quiver,
Swaying to the rhythm in an enraptured shiver.
Your percussive power, a pulse in the air,
Like nature's heartbeat, a reminder fair,
Of forces unseen, yet forever profound,
Majestic vibrations that shake the ground.
Through lightning's flash, and rain's gentle kiss,
Brontide commands existence with sheer bliss,
Igniting the senses in a tempest of sound,
A dance of elements, nature's playground.
Oh, Brontide, your magnitude cannot be contained,
Unleashed ambience, wild and unrestrained,
From mountains to oceans, your voice shall persist,
In melodies of thunder that none can resist.
So, let your rhythm guide the weary souls,
In awe and wonder, as the thunder rolls,
For in your essence, lies a world's story,
A symphony of life, a glimpse of glory.

Aesthete

In the realm of beauty, where dreams entwine,
Resides a soul, a fervent aesthete divine.
With eyes like mirrors, reflecting grace,
They seek the sublime in every place.
Aesthete, a seeker, a lover of arts,
With fingertips that touch the finest parts,
They dance through galleries, breathlessly swoon,
In the presence of beauty, their heart's festooned.
In sunsets painted with hues of gold,
Or moonlit nights where mysteries unfold,
The aesthete finds solace, finds their trace,
In every stroke, in every embrace.
Through melodies that whisper in the breeze,
Or written words that unravel with such ease,
They find harmony in the rhythms of life,
In symphonies that drown away the strife.
With each brushstroke, a story is told,
Aesthete's heart unearths what molds,
Their vision, a lens, where spirits seep,
Creating worlds, unveiling secrets deep.
In gardens adorned with blossoms fair,
Or poetry that weaves tales beyond compare,
Their senses awaken, their spirits ignite,
Transcending boundaries, taking flight.
But, dear aesthete, your soul is not confined,
To canvases or verses, you're inclined,
To see the beauty in each passing day,

In the mundane, you unearth a bouquet.
For the world, like a symphony, is your muse,
With colors and textures, it will amuse,
Your heart that beats to the rhythm of art,
Aesthete, may your passion never depart.
So, let your eyes forever seek the sublime,
And let your soul bask in beauty's chime,
For you, dear aesthete, are a vessel of grace,
A poet of life, painting smiles on every face.

Sophrosyne

In the realm of tranquil grace, she resides,
Sophrosyne, the essence of balance untamed.
A silent symphony of steadfast strength,
Her spirit dances upon the waves of wisdom.
With eyes that mirror the serenity of dawn,
She weaves a cadence of harmony divine.
In every breath, a tender serenade,
Guiding hearts to find solace in her embrace.
Like a gentle whisper, she calls from within,
A reminder to seek virtue, to find peace.
Oceans of desires rush and roar all around,
Yet she stands firm, her essence never wavers.
In her presence, chaos quiets its storm,
And hasty passions retreat with humble grace.
For Sophrosyne, the guardian of the soul,
Does nurture our spirit, emboldens our quest.
In the realm of tranquil grace, let us dwell,
Seeking solace in her tranquil embrace.
For in her arms, true contentment resides,
And the tumultuous world finds momentary cease.
Oh, Sophrosyne, ephemeral and ever true,
Guide us to find the wisdom within,
To live in harmony, to be in tune,
With the symphony of our souls' gentle hum.

Elysian

In the realm of dreams, where shadows blend,
Lies a land untouched by mortal sin,
Elysian, a paradise untamed,
Where seraphs dance and ethereal beings reign.
In Elysian's meadows of golden hue,
Where fragrant blooms in vibrant hues,
The air is filled with celestial song,
As whispers of harmony gently throng.
Through emerald forests, the rivers wind,
Their crystal waters, a treasure to find,
Reflecting the skies in shimmering grace,
Mirrors of peace, where troubles efface.
Oh, Elysian! A sanctuary of peace,
Where every heartbeat finds sweet release,
Where weary souls find solace and rest,
In your embrace, they are forever blessed.
In this haven, time loses its hold,
And memories of pain turn soft and old,
As souls rejoice in eternal embrace,
In Elysian's beauty, a sacred space.
But alas, Elysian remains untamed,
A distant realm to which few are named,
And yet, within each heart, a spark resides,
A glimmer of hope, where paradise abides.
So, let us seek Elysian's divine light,
In every moment, hold its promise tight,
For within our souls, this essence lies,

Eternity's whispers, an eternal prize.
May Elysian's beauty guide our way,
In every choice, in each new day,
And may we find, in our lives so brief,
A touch of heaven, a taste of Elysian's splendor and peace.

Mångata

In the twilight's tender glow, where golden hues reside,
There in the vast celestial canvas, a whispered dream collides,
A ribbon of enchantment, where land and water blend,
Mångata dances on the waves, an ethereal message to send.
Oh, Mångata, celestial pathway of shimmering light,
You guide us through the depths of night, soothing our hearts' plight,
A silver bridge betwixt the realms, a glimpse of the divine,
Your gentle touch upon the sea forever shall be mine.
As nightfall's velvet cloak unfurls, a tapestry of stars,
Mångata paints a wistful tale, of love that leaves no scars,
Beyond the reach of mortal eyes, a cosmic rendezvous,
You mirror the moon's tender kiss, in a blissful rendezvous.
A reflection of serenity, you hold secrets yet untold,
Mångata, mystical mirror, your beauty does unfold,
Your luminescence, soft and calm, filling the night with grace,
Whispers of forgotten dreams, a longing to embrace.
In quiet moments of solace, when hearts are worn and tired,
Mångata, you become a balm, with dreams of hope inspired,
You beckon us to wander, to a realm beyond our sight,
Where magic dwells and dreams take flight, bathed in your gentle light.
So let us drift upon your waves, as dreamers often do,
Mångata, weave your moonlit spell, and let our spirits renew,
In your embrace, we find solace, a tranquil, sacred shore,
Where dreams meet reality, and souls forever explore.

Koi No Yokan

In the realm of love, there lies a mystic hue,
A spark, a knowing, felt by me and you.
Koi no yokan, a tender ember's glow,
Foreboding whispers of love's seeds to sow.
Like ripples on a pond, the heart's gentle dance,
We sense destiny's brushstroke, this love's chance.
Unseen, yet palpable, in the air it drifts,
Our souls entwined, as destiny uplifts.
In moments stolen, eyes silently speak,
Words unspoken, love's language oh so meek.
In every glance, a tale of love untold,
A koi no yokan, a truth that soon unfolds.
Our hands may brush, igniting flames within,
As we venture close to love's sacred inn.
The universe conspires to whisper and nudge,
Koi no yokan, where love's dance we begrudge.
With each passing day, the yearning grows,
A pull that cannot be explained, it shows.
In dreams and waking hours, our spirits intertwine,
Koi no yokan, a love firmly divine.
For love, oh love, a language dares not state,
Yet resonates deeply, amidst love's fate.
Koi no yokan, a knowing shall endure,
The whisper of love's song, forever pure.
So let us embrace this fate, ever true,
Koi no yokan, the love that binds me to you.
For in our hearts, a love shall forever reside,

IGNATIUS MAXIMUS JOHN AND GRACE LALRINPARI HAUZEL

A flame that burns, unwavering, side by side.

Abditory

A place of peace and quiet,
Where the world cannot intrude,
A place to think and ponder,
And let your thoughts be freed.
A place to read and write,
Or simply gaze out the window,
A place to be alone,
And forget your troubles for a while.
A place of solitude,
Where you can be yourself,
A place to relax and unwind,
And let your worries melt away.
A place of refuge,
Where you can escape the everyday,
A place to find your inner peace,
And be at one with yourself.
Abditory,
A place of sanctuary,
A place where you can be free.

Flawsome

I am not perfect,
That's for sure.
I have my flaws,
And I know they're there.
But I'm not ashamed of them,
Not anymore.
I've learned to embrace them,
And even love them some more.
Because my flaws make me who I am,
They make me unique.
They give me character,
And they make me beautiful.
So I'm not perfect,
But I'm flawsome.
And I wouldn't have it any other way.
I'm Flawsome
I'm not afraid to be myself,
Even if I'm not perfect.
I know that my flaws make me who I am,
And I wouldn't change a thing.
I'm flawed, but I'm also beautiful.
I'm unique, and I'm special.
I'm flawsome, and I'm proud of it.
So if you're feeling down about your flaws,
Just remember that you're not alone.
We all have our flaws,
But that's what makes us human.

So embrace your flaws,
And love yourself for who you are.
Because you're flawsome,
And that's something to be proud of.

Datsuzoku

To escape the daily grind,
To break free from the routine,
To find a place of peace and quiet,
Where I can be me.
To wander through the forest,
To breathe the fresh air,
To listen to the birdsong,
To feel the sun on my skin.
To sit by the river,
To watch the water flow,
To let my thoughts drift away,
To be at one with nature.
To be free from the noise,
To be free from the stress,
To be free from the expectations,
To be Datsuzoku.
To be Datsuzoku
Is to be free,
To be yourself,
To be at peace,
To be happy.
It is to find your own way,
To follow your own path,
To live your own life,
To be Datsuzoku.

Vacilando

To linger, to pause,
To take a moment to breathe,
To appreciate the journey,
Not just the destination.
To wander aimlessly,
With no particular goal in mind,
To simply be present,
In the moment.
To savor the simple things,
The taste of a good meal,
The sound of laughter,
The smell of flowers.
To be open to new experiences,
To let go of expectations,
To be Vacilando.
To be Vacilando
Is to be in the flow,
To be at peace with yourself,
To be content with the unknown,
To be free.
It is to live in the moment,
To be present in your life,
To be grateful for what you have,
To be Vacilando.
Vacilando
Is a state of being,
A way of life,

A journey of discovery,
A path to happiness.
So let's all Vacilando,
And enjoy the ride.

Komorebi

Golden rays of light
Dance through vibrant green leaves,
Komorebi's grace.
Shadows and whispers,
Nature's gentle orchestra,
Komorebi's hush.
Silent canopy,
Nature's stained glass masterpiece,
Komorebi's art.

Metanoia

Metanoia, a journey of the soul,
A transformation that makes us whole.
It is the turning of our inner gaze,
A shift in perspective, a change of ways.
From darkness to light, we seek to find,
The truth that lies within our mind.
With open hearts and open eyes,
We let go of old beliefs and lies.
Metanoia, a dance of the spirit,
A chance to grow, to evolve, to inherit,
The wisdom that comes from deep within,
As we shed our old skin, we begin.
To question the world and question ourselves,
To explore the depths where true healing dwells.
In this sacred space of self-reflection,
We find liberation, a new direction.
Metanoia, a surrendering of ego's hold,
A release of attachments that once controlled.
We embrace the unknown, the uncertain,
And in this surrender, we find our true curtain.
To step into the flow of life's river,
To trust in the process, to let go and deliver.
Our hearts to the rhythm of the divine,
In this surrender, our souls intertwine.
Metanoia, a rebirth of the soul,
A letting go of what no longer serves our whole.
In this awakening, we find our purpose,

A calling that ignites our inner furnace.
To live with passion, with love and grace,
To embrace each moment, to run life's race.
Metanoia, a journey that never ends,
For it is through growth that our soul transcends.

Peregrinate

Peregrinate, a wanderer's quest,
To roam the Earth, to be truly blessed.
With feet that tread on unfamiliar ground,
A nomad's spirit, forever unbound.
Through mountains and valleys, across the seas,
In search of beauty, in search of peace.
To leave behind the comforts of home,
And let the world's wonders freely roam.
Peregrinate, a journey of the soul,
To find oneself in places untold.
In ancient ruins and bustling streets,
In every encounter, a new heartbeat.
With open eyes and open mind,
We leave our fears and doubts behind.
For in the unknown, we find our strength,
And discover the treasures of great length.
Peregrinate, a dance with the unknown,
A chance to grow, to truly be shown.
The vastness of this world, so grand,
As we explore, hand in hand.
To meet strangers who become dear friends,
To learn from cultures that never ends.
Peregrinate, a tapestry of stories,
Weaved by the hands of those who seek glories.
In each step taken, a lesson learned,
In each destination, a new page turned.
For peregrination is more than just travel,

It's a way of life that unravels.
The mysteries of this world we share,
The beauty that's found everywhere.
So let us peregrinate, with hearts alight,
For in this journey, we truly take flight.

Perambulate

Perambulate, a gentle stroll,
To wander aimlessly, to let time unfold.
With leisurely steps on familiar paths,
Exploring the world in a peaceful dance.
Through parks and gardens, down quiet lanes,
In search of solace, in search of gains.
To leave behind the chaos of the day,
And let the mind wander, freely sway.
Perambulate, a journey of the mind,
To find tranquility, to leave worries behind.
In nature's embrace and city streets,
In every moment, a sense of retreat.
With unhurried pace and mindful gaze,
We savor the beauty in simple ways.
For in the familiar, we find our peace,
And discover the joys that never cease.
Perambulate, a conversation with oneself,
A chance to reflect, to find inner wealth.
The simplicity of life, so profound,
As we meander, thoughts unbound.
To notice the details often missed,
To appreciate the moments that persist.
Perambulate, a symphony of serenity,
Played by the rhythm of each step's melody.
In each stride taken, a moment seized,
In each destination, a sense of ease.
For perambulation is more than just a walk,

It's a way of being, a chance to talk.
With oneself and the world around,
To find harmony in every sound.
So let us perambulate, with hearts at ease,
For in this journey, we find true peace.

Peripatetic

Strolling through the world,
Peripatetic's stride,
Wisdom from the road.
Wandering footsteps,
Seeking knowledge, truth, and light,
Peripatetic.
Journey ever on,
In perpetual motion,
Peripatetic soul.

Shinrin-yoku

Beneath ancient trees,
Whispering leaves calm the soul,
Forest bathes my mind.
Dappled sunlight shines,
Nature's harmony echoes,
Inhale, exhale peace.
Earth's embrace enfolds,
Awakened senses rejoice,
Nature heals my heart.

Shinrabansho

Shinrabansho shines,
Nature's essence entwined souls,
Bound in universe.
Mystic energy,
Flowing through every being,
Shinrabansho's gift.
Harmony unfolds,
Shinrabansho's wisdom blooms,
Peace whispers softly.

Gadabout

A gadabout, always on the go,
Roaming round without a care
Experiencing sights and moments galore,
Adventures without a spare
Nary a worry in sight,
Merrily through the days
Living with the utmost delight,
In moments in every phase
A wanderer does not tackle a plan,
To any sort of task
A gadabout knows well what she can,
And gets her wishes fast
No matter the ebb and tide,
A gadabout will still explore
For they know that if they can't decide,
All paths hold something more

Hiraeth

Longing for a home I know not.
A place where I do not belong.
A quiet comfort that I cannot touch.
Hoping for a faint hum in the air
That I can call my own.
A gentle embrace, that I miss so much.
Hiraeth, the feeling of missing
The things I can't go back to
The things I so desperately long for.
My heart feels true nostalgia,
Searching for a place to call my own
But I instead, sigh alone.
Hiraeth, my melancholic companion
The sorrow of not belonging
The emotion that travels with me wherever I go.

Toska

Oh to feel the pain of Toska,
A sensation that no one can explain.
As though a wound of the heart,
Numbing and deep.
An emptiness that can swallow a soul,
A sorrow that eats away at the whole.
The silent screams with a face of apathy,
That kills all hope though mysteriously.
What would bring a heart to this state?
A pain that brings a frightful fate.
A torturous surrender gripping the mind,
Till one can no longer bear the bind.
A torment that speaks without words,
An end in sight no one can hear.
But a comforting embrace in the soul's night,
The tide rising with the feeling of Toska's might.

Dépaysement

The sky I see is different there
The scents and smells do not compare
The food is strange, the language too
For more than a few weeks I do not do
Traveling abroad and feeling lost
Not quite at home like comfort crossed
New expectation, new style of life
Uncertainty might cause some strife
But with strong will I stand to look
Before my eyes, a unique brochure
Exploring the culture that has grown
Taking pictures, never to be cloned
A winding path of dépaysement
Away from home, but gaining new intent
Watched by curious eye, but prepared bravery
A world of new, different but the same.

Dès Vu

My memories are cloaked in fog,
My memories, a dense-walled bog
Submerged secrets and lost potential,
Of a life I cannot remember or ascensional.
My recollection is warped and blue,
Vague and distant, like a distant hue.
This moment I'm distracted and sidelined
This is a feeling I know all too well, its called dèjà vu.
My heart feels heavy with an unknown remorse,
A feeling of uneasiness without an identified cause.
The future is no clearer, yet I fear the situation will remain
This feeling of deja vu, I can't shake it again.
This feeling will remain until the day
When I find out what I already knew that day
When I realize that this is my own life
The uncertainty will not remain, Dès vu my only strife.

Cynefin

Cynefin is where I find my peace
A tranquil melody envelopes me
It's a stillness that can't be found anywhere else
A feeling of comfort and of rest
I wander through the meadow's low
Grazing freely through the shade
The beauty of this land I know
My heart and mind has time to fade
The autumn air is gently cool
Fanning wings as if to soothe
And I pause for just a moment, to take in its view
The picturesque scene of Cynefin so true
Though I may roam this place one more day
My spirit never leaves this place
A remembrance of beauty and peace I'll take away
As I wander out of Cynefin's grace.

Safarnama

Flying everywhere, mountains and plains,
Travelling around like exotic birds,
Climbing the slopes covered in snow,
Discovering exotic places on the go.
Roaming around the streets of Morocco,
Vast gardens and towers I espied,
Walking the alleys of every city,
Mesmerizing beauty of countryside.
Exploring Venice's winding canals,
Picturesque bridges and houses so small,
Feasting my eyes on Sicily's beauty,
Tasting their pizza with lots of yummy.
Every country so unique in its own,
A feast to soul, mind and heart,
Each place so different, so peculiar,
I shall love to return and start.

Saudade

My heart aches in unspoken desire,
Saudade, a longing I hold inside.
A pain with no desired cure
A love lost in the tide.
Memories that haunt, reminders of a past
Alone, I cry, for what could not last.
Aching, I go through the days
Silently, wishing I could make it okay.
The emptiness inside just grows
The deeper in thought I go.
My heart forever aching,
As what was subsides to nothing, showing
The space a lost love has left
The depths of saudade I cannot forget.
But with resilience in my heart, I try
To rise up with no further cry.

Yūgen

An emotion that can't quite be seen,
A feeling that's beyond belief.
Yūgen is something none can define
Between deep shadows and ancient scenes.
The beauty of an ethereal chance,
A hint of awe that feels so strange.
The evocation of a thousand stars,
A hidden captivation in every heart.
Where the stars shine brightest in the night,
Where the quiet sound of rain reveals.
A world where moments never end,
Yūgen awakens the soul and transcends.

Wabi-Sabi

The flawed, natural beauty of wabi-sabi,
So often overlooked in our hurried lives.
Ah the beauty of things that are worn, torn and cracked.
The years of energy and life seen through these objects that we can't deny.
A bowl holds many stories,
Of hands that shaped and held it,
A reminder of simpler times
When things moved ever so slowly through life.
The broken bits of a teacup,
Show the experience of it's life.
Living and expanding it's story
A beacon of love, acceptance and peace.
It the cracks and imperfections of life,
That we come to admire,
The beauty of ever-changing life
That can't be captured in time.

Ukiyo

Floating world of bliss
Cherry blossoms paint the air
Dreams dance on the breeze
Geisha's gentle grace
In shimmering silk they sway
Ukiyo's embrace
Tea ceremonies
Calmly sipping moments passed
Ukiyo unfolds

Ikigai

Finding true purpose,
Ikigai reveals path,
Heart and soul aligned.
Passion, skill, value,
Ikigai intertwines them,
Flowing with meaning.
In harmony's embrace,
Ikigai's sweet melody,
Life's symphony plays.

Apprivoise

In her hands, the brush,
With delicate strokes she creates,
Art breathes, comes alive.
Whispers of music,
Flow through her skilled fingertips,
Dancing notes take flight.
Through Apprivoise's touch,
Canvas, clay, and tales find voice,
Transformed, mesmerized.

Còsagach

Warm crackling fire,
Cozy blanket of comfort,
Còsagach's embrace.
Soft woolen textures,
Snuggled in a rustic nook,
Còsagach solace.
Whispering winter,
Candle's flickering embrace,
Còsagach's peace.

Ataraxia

In the realm of tranquil repose,
Where serenity gracefully flows,
Dwells Ataraxia, gentle and rare,
A refuge from life's ceaseless snare.
In this oasis of seraphic dreams,
Where stillness reigns, it redeems,
A hallowed space where all fears calm,
And troubled thoughts find soothing balm.
Ataraxia whispers in the wind,
A melody of solace, a respite, a friend,
Inviting weary souls to rest,
And unravel the knots within their chest.
Oh, how the world can swiftly spin,
With chaos and noise that dwell within,
But in Ataraxia's embrace so profound,
One finds peace, tranquility unbound.
The mind unburdens its heavy load,
And moments of clarity effortlessly unfold,
Like silver streams that gently cascade,
Leaving no room for worries to pervade.
Oh, Ataraxia, an ethereal grace,
Guiding light in life's turbulent race,
Through your gentle touch, we dare to be free,
Lost in the sweet embrace of harmony.
So let us seek thy sacred shores,
When life's storms rage and turmoil roars,
For within Ataraxia, we find release,

And in surrender, true inner peace.

Absquatulate

In a realm where words curve and dance,
Where language weaves a transcendent trance,
A tale I shall spin, both wild and grand,
Of a word that leaps from the poet's hand.
Absquatulate, with a flourish it lands,
A verb so rare, like grains of golden sands,
It tells a tale of a daring departure,
Of vanishing minds and hearts in rupture.
Imagine a soul, restless and untamed,
Yearning to break free, a spirit unclaimed,
Through tempestuous winds and skies of blue,
It seeks escape, with a hunger anew.
Absquatulate, it whispers with grace,
A whispered promise, a secret embrace,
To flee complacency's invisible chains,
And venture forth where no map ever gains.
With nimble feet, it dances through time,
Beguiling our hearts with a rhythm so prime,
A rebel within, it beckons to trace,
Paths of defiance, with style and grace.
Like the wind on the fields, it takes flight,
Chasing dreams and the vastness of night,
Absquatulate! The call echoes wide,
Inviting us all, to traverse the tide.
The traveler within, awakened with care,
In every heartbeat, a dare to declare,
To wander, explore, and defy the mundane,

With Absquatulate, liberation shall reign.
So, let us embrace this delightfully rare,
And journey beyond the ordinary's lair,
For true liberation, we shall translate,
Through Absquatulate, let's liberate!

www.ingramcontent.com/pod-product-compliance
Lightning Source LLC
Chambersburg PA
CBHW051803130726
47987CB00003B/1092